James Amaziah Whitney

The Patent Office and the Problem of Reform

James Amaziah Whitney

The Patent Office and the Problem of Reform

ISBN/EAN: 9783337296360

Printed in Europe, USA, Canada, Australia, Japan

Cover: Foto ©Lupo / pixelio.de

More available books at **www.hansebooks.com**

THE PATENT OFFICE

AND

THE PROBLEM OF REFORM

BY

JAMES A. WHITNEY, LL. D.,

Counselor at Law.

*WITH AN APPENDIX OF PRACTICAL ADVICE TO
INVENTORS AND PATENTEES.*

BY THE SAME AUTHOR :

In Preparation.

RIGHTS AND PRIVILEGES OF MANUFACTURERS UNDER
STATE AND NATIONAL TRADE MARK LAWS.

ISSUED FROM

United States and Foreign Patent Agency Offices, Rooms 430 and 431, Temple Court,
cor. Beekman and Nassau Streets. New York City.

Applications for Patents in all countries where Patents are granted ; Registration of Trade Marks
in all countries where Trade Marks are registered ; and all business in the United
States Patent Office prosecuted with thoroughness and dispatch.

PREFACE.

THIS brochure is the result of more than thirty years' familiarity with the practice and procedure of the Patent Office and the law as applicable thereto. While it goes without saying that a subject which relates so directly to the industrial welfare of the country should be considered in a temperate and judicial manner, it by no means follows that convictions born of accurate knowledge, and fostered by long and careful reflection, should not be forcibly expressed. The keynote to the following pages is found in the propositions that inventors are benefactors of the human race, that civilization in all its better aspects has become what it is through their efforts ; that the law of patents is based upon justice as promotive of the public welfare ; that inventors go before the Patent Office as a matter of right, and not as a matter of favor ; that whatever, in the practice of the Patent Office or in its administration of the law, discriminates against the true interests of inventors should be reprobated and reformed ; and that defects in the law itself should be remedied by legislation so firmly and so clearly expressed, that error in its interpretation or mistake in its application may become practically impossible.

The appendix comprises suggestions which, it is thought, may, even to experienced inventors, be of some value ; but which are more especially intended for the guidance of those who are novices in threading the useful paths of industrial and scientific improvement. While the Patent Office falls short, in many ways, of ideal perfection, it is not to be denied that its work would be materially facilitated, and justice to applicants be greatly promoted, if inventors themselves were, as a rule, more systematic in the development of their ideas, and more attentive to legal requirements and to rules of practice in the presentation and prosecution of their cases. It is for the purpose of inciting to effort in this direction that the appendix has been prepared for perusal in connection with that larger portion of these pages which relates to modification of the patent law, and reform in the organization of the patent office.

JAMES A. WHITNEY.

TEMPLE COURT, NEW YORK CITY
June, 1896.

THE PATENT OFFICE AND THE PROBLEM OF REFORM.

The Moral and Legal Rights of Inventors.

THE patent law of the United States rests upon positive statute. Its administration does not depend upon an inherent power of the executive, as was originally the case under English law.

The moral right of an inventor to a patent is based upon a primary principle of justice, viz.: that if he gives the public a valuable improvement, the public ought to pay him for it ; and upon the simple business principle that the easiest way for the public to pay him is to let him have the chance to make as much out of it as he can by its exclusive manufacture, sale, and use for a limited time. In ethics, this is all that there is of the law of patents. It is enough. It is primitive justice and simple common sense.

The legal right of an inventor to a patent rests, as just remarked, upon enacted law. The public has clothed the government with the power to grant patents. This power is embodied in a paragraph of the Constitution, and has been effectuated through a succession of statutes which extend, in this country, over a period of more than a hundred years. Through them, as by a process of evolution, our present system, with all its merits and demerits, has been formulated. The law has been changed from time to time to remedy deficiencies, real or imagined. In some respects it has been improved, in others it has retrograded. The law, as it stands upon the pages of the Revised Statutes of the United States, is upon its face fair toward the inventor and just toward the public.

The Patent Office is, *in theory*, an ideal institution. The law, as understood and administered, is composed of the written statutes, their interpretation by the courts, and the understanding of that interpretation by the officials of the Patent Office. By the time the law gets around to the inventor, the latter not infrequently laments the mysterious dispensations of jurisprudence when filtered through the aggregated mentalities of a government bureau.

In its practical results upon inventors and inventions, and consequently upon industries, our patent system, which has sometimes been asserted to be the best in the world, is in many respects the worst. It is doubtful whether there is another civilized country which assumes to reward its inventors, where the rights of the latter are so restricted by formalism, red tape, and the arbitrariness of unchecked authority. That this is true is primarily due to the system of examinations in the Patent Office ; to the opportunities for irresponsible action on the part of Examiners, and to the disproportion between the work to be done and the force available to do it.

To afford a fair idea of this, it may be worth while to note the usual experience of an application before the Patent Office. In so doing we assume the application to have been properly prepared, its specification sufficiently lucid, its claims definite and clear, its drawings sharply defined, and its formal papers correct.* All these go in the first instance, to officials whose duty it is to see that all are in proper form. It sometimes happens that an unnecessarily technical point is here raised, but usually there is no trouble at this initial stage, provided, of course, that the applicant has properly complied with the reasonable statutory and official rules.

Inventions, under the classification adopted in the Patent Office, are divided into classes, which in their turn are divided into subclasses. Each division includes a class, and is placed under the control of a primary or, as he is sometimes termed, a principal

---

* Examiners may, *and should*, insist that applications be drawn with due regard to the rules of the Patent Office, and in such manner as to clearly disclose the invention and define what it is. It is not to be denied that the labor of Examiners would be materially diminished, the character of their work enhanced, and, it may be, their judicial discretion exercised with less asperity, if they were not so much annoyed by carelessness and incompetence displayed in the preparation of many of the cases brought before them. There are probably thousands of applications filed every year in which the slip-shod work of the specification-writer places a heavy tax on the time and patience of the Primary Examiners and their assistants. How this may be rectified is a subject entirely distinct and apart from that considered in the text. Every statement and reference comprised in the latter is to be understood as relating only to cases in which reasonable care and competent attainments have been brought to bear in the preparation of specifications, claims, drawings, and formal papers, and in which the applications have been filed in exact accordance with the rules of law and practice.

Examiner. The latter has several assistants. When the application has been found to be regular in form, and the first government fee has been paid, the case is sent to that Examiner who has charge of the class of inventions to which the Improvement relates, and whose duty it is to examine it upon the merits, and to cite any previous machine, process, composition, or other matter, which in his judgment should prevent the allowance of the claims. The matters thus referred to by the Examiner as against the application are termed "references," in the current phrase of the Patent Office.

After a delay which varies with the different divisions, the application is reached "in its order" for examination. It is precisely at this point in its existence that the vicissitudes of the application are likely to begin ; where often are initiated experiences which make the inventor sigh, and not infrequently lead the patent attorney to vigorous expressions of discontent.

Opportunities for Unjustifiable Treatment of Inventors under the Present System.

The Akhoond of Swat is not more absolute within his renowned dominion than is a Primary Examiner in control of a division who chooses to place his own notions ahead of his official duty. There is, in fact, no functionary anywhere (with one solitary exception, that exception being an "Assistant Examiner-in-charge)" who is liable to be afflicted with so altitudinous a consciousness of personal exaltation, or through whom this weakness of human nature may do more harm. He may reject an application upon an alleged reference which has nothing to do with the case, and when the applicant has carefully demonstrated this, he may repeat his action, with the result of compelling an appeal, with additional expense, to the Board of Examiners-in-Chief. If overruled by the latter, he may "discover" a new reference which has been "accidently overlooked," and reject the case again, thus placing before the applicant the alternative of further appeal and additional outlay, or of abandoning his application altogether. He may embarrass an application by absurd verbal criticisms, which the applicant or his representative is expected to meet with an aspect of submissive deference and grave respect,* or

* This expectation is, however, occasionally the source of disappointment to an Examiner. Before the Patent-Office, a clear understanding of the subject, on the

may make requirements not expected nor required by other Examiners, and which may be futile upon their face, and may be irremediable in their results, and which cause annoyance and delay.

Cases are not unknown where applications that, with proper regard to the rights of the inventor, could have been passed to issue in two or three months, have been kept dangling before the Patent Office for as many years, and this, by the manifestly intentional perversity of an Examiner.

An Examiner may do all this, and there is practically no remedy for it. He may do even worse than this, and equally without reparation. He may allow the application, when, in fact, there is an available reference which should defeat it, and which renders the patent invalid if granted. The time devoted to technicalities by an Examiner is, of course, just so much abstracted from that available for legitimate work, and an official who devotes his energies to obstructing the just claims of inventors, is commonly of too small a caliber to be able to do much else. Under the present system, therefore, an ill-disposed Examiner not only has it in his power to deny rights to those who are entitled to them, but is also likely to accord rights to those who have no lawful claim to them. It is no benefit to an inventor to receive a patent which is clearly anticipated in the prior state of the art. Such a patent is a delusion and a snare, a trap to the patentee, and a wrong to the public.

The writer is informed, but has no personal familiarity with the affair, that one Examiner, a " first Assistant," has kept a regular list of those attorneys who have offended his sense of personal importance with the avowed object of revenging his egoistic animosities by his official action.

It is easy to perceive that a system in which such a condition of affairs is even possible, must be repugnant to all proper ideas of administrative justice, and must afford opportunities for many and great abuses.

It is not to be assumed that all, or a majority, of the Examining corps are of the offensive type above indicated. A very large majority of the Examiners are men who desire to do justice to inventors without doing injustice to the public. But it should be

part of the applicant or his representative, a firm and judicious insistence in the assertion of apparent rights, and a careful regard for legal requirements and official proprieties, are the foundations of success.

sufficient to condemn the present system that possibilities such as have been referred to actually exist. When it is considered that the expense of an Appeal from an erroneous action of a Primary Examiner necessitates not only delay, but also the expenditure of a government fee, and, usually, an extra attorney fee, the hardship of a wrongful decision by a Primary Examiner is at once apparent. Ordinarily an appeal may be considered as practically doubling the expense of applying for a patent. Very frequently, too, the action of an Examiner leads an inventor to so modify his claims as to avoid clashing with an objection urged by the Examiner, even though it may unduly narrow the patent when issued, and thus afford immunity to those who may invade the invention without infringing the claims. The extent to which this has been carried may be inferred from the number of reissues granted during the period when reissues were regarded with favor, a period which covered about forty years. In nearly every instance the reissue was sought for the purpose of broadening the claim beyond what had been originally allowed by the Patent Office, and the allowance of the reissue was evidence that this was the case. They numbered upward of ten thousand. There is no reason to suppose that the ratio of patents which cover less than the inventor is entitled to is any less at the present time.

A further evil result of the present system arises from the fact that whatever an Examiner chooses to assert against an invention, no matter how futile or erroneous it may be, goes into the record of the application for permanent preservation. This record may thus be made to contain practically all the material for a ready-made brief in behalf of an infringer of the patent, the record being open to public inspection as soon as the patent has issued. It is thus possible for an Examiner to blacken a patent in advance, and for this blackening to remain as long as the patent exists. This, of course, may in many cases impa the value of the patent, even when the Examiner's theory and objections have been totally over-ruled within the Patent Office, and the patent issued over his head and in spite of him. Another defect of existing law and practice lies in the fact that there are no adequate means by which an obstinate or perverse Examiner can be compelled to properly respect the decisions of the Appellate Tribunal, beyond the specific case in which his action has been reversed. It is true that an

Examiner is commonly chary of directly colliding with a decision or a rule of practice established by the Commissioner in person. But an Examiner of the type indicated has frequently a decided talent—it may be the only one he possesses—of drawing minute and evasive distinctions, which afford color of keeping within the letter of the decision or of the rule, as the case may be. Even in instances where these are clearly disregarded, the chances are that the matter may not come to the personal knowledge of the Commissioner. As concerns reversals of an Examiner's decision by the Board of Examiners-in-Chief, an Examiner may have been overruled by this tribunal in a dozen different cases involving the same principle of practice or interpretation. He is compelled to respect the decision of the Board in each of them, but there is nothing to prevent him from disregarding their authority as precedents in the very next case that comes before him. As if to accentuate the enforced submission of an applicant to the arbitrary decrees of a Primary Examiner, the statute provides that no appeal can be taken to the Board until the claim has been twice acted upon by the Primary Examiner. It may be perfectly apparent to the applicant that the Examiner will persist in his action. Nevertheless, he must ask for a further consideration. There is no reason for this in justice or equity.

When we consider the almost colossal value of some inventions to the public, the beneficent intent of the statute to afford complete protection to meritorious inventors, and the extent to which the fortunes of the latter depend upon proper recognition of their claims, it is apparent that the power and authority of a Primary Examiner over the rights of applicants is greater than ought to be confided to any one official where it is at all possible to avoid it.

And more than this ! The system of Examination is the same now as thirty years ago. There are conceded objections to which, thus far, in these pages no allusion has been made. These were set-forth in cogent terms as long ago as 1872 by the then Commissioner of Patents. Among other things he said :

"There being no authoritative review of the work of the Examiners, there is no protection against hasty and careless examinations, and, what is still worse, the door is thrown wide open to incessant importunings and to corrupt influences of every kind."

After disclaiming any suspicion as to the personal integrity of any Examiner, he continued as follows :

"The present corps consists of men of high character and ability, but I deem it unnecessary and unwise that interests of such importance should be thus exposed, resting solely upon the integrity of a single officer. Very large amounts are often involved in these decisions. Dishonest applicants, it may be presumed, are ready to pay very liberally for patents when they cannot get them without, and outside parties adversely interested can often afford equal liberality to secure final rejections."

Apparently believing that even this strong language did not adequately cover the facts relative to the system, the said Commissioner continued as follows :

"The present organization furnishing no certain check to such fraud, and the Commissioner having no basis but the established integrity of the Examiners upon which to deny its existence, corruption is freely and almost daily charged, and by many fully believed. The consequence is that the value of preliminary examinations is seriously affected, and public confidence in the validity of patents is much less than it should be. It is doubtful whether in any other bureau or department of the Government equal interests are intrusted to the examination and final decision of a single person, with practically no check against carelessness, ignorance, and fraud."

Such was the deliberate language of a Commissioner of Patents, speaking in his official capacity, and with a vigor of expression unusual in official reports. Comment appears to be entirely unnecessary, and the necessity of reform in the interest of the public to be apparent beyond a peradventure. "*Practically no check against carelessness, ignorance, and fraud.*" Such was the characterization of this system twenty-four years ago by the head of the Patent Office. The system has not been changed since then. It would be futile to inquire why there has been no change. It is high time that the inventors and manufacturers of the country roused themselves to see to it, that a change is made, and, that right speedily.

No Remedy Except by Radical Modification of the System.

While, as has just been implied, the obstacles thrown in an inventor's way may be, and not infrequently are, due to arbitrary and unjustifiable disregard of his rights by Examiners, such examples are paralleled by those arising from conditions which practically inhibit Examiners from that full and careful performance of their duties which is contemplated by the law, and which the inventor has a right to expect from the Government. This may be best illustrated by an example recently arising in the practice of the writer, who filed charges against an Examiner for neglect in failing to cite all the references relied upon in rejecting an application before an Appeal was taken, and for disregarding an argument which would have shown the Examiner that he was in error concerning a reference. In justification the Examiner replied, referring to the charges (the italics are ours), as follows :

" The first ground is in not citing the best references in rejection of the case.* *This the Examiner acknowledges to be the case*, and did so on the record. Applicant's attorney goes on at length to descant on a certain argument filed by him which he claims would have clearly shown the Examiner his error. *No doubt this is true.* The attorney has been practicing long enough before the office to know that a principal Examiner, having six assistants, *and having an average of six hundred cases a month* reported to him, cannot personally read arguments in these cases. He must depend for the proper presentation of the case upon his assistants."

In another part of his reply addressed to the Commissioner, the Examiner said :

" Your Honor is perfectly familiar with the amount of work we have, and applicant's case has not been delayed any more than anybody else's. It was taken up in its due order. I wish further to state in this connection, but for the attorney's benefit, that for some time past I have been working overtime, doing work at home, in order that the work should not fall into arrears. Probably, upon learning this, the attorney will be more lenient in his judgment, both as to the mistake and the lapse of time."

It appears from this that an argument which would have shown the Examiner his error was ignored entirely. It will, probably, not be denied that it was the proper business of some person to read and to understand the argument which was filed in behalf of the inventor, and which was directly responsive to the Examiner's action in the case. Yet the Patent Office admits that the Primary

---

* The Examiner's grammar, it will be noticed, is a little shaky. This, however, does not detract from the value of the evidence afforded by his statement.

Examiner, who was responsible for the proper conduct of the examination, did not read it, and by reason of the pressure of work upon him could not be expected to read it. It does not appear that any of his assistants did read it. No matter what the cause or explanation of this, it is not open to question that no such occurrence ought to be possible in the examination of an application. An inventor is entitled to treatment quite different from this when he comes before the Patent Office to ask for protection under the law. In the case mentioned, the statement of the patent official amounts simply to this : that the Examiner responsible for that division could not attend to the examination of the case, but was compelled to leave it to an assistant, and that the latter paid no attention to the argument. It further appears from the Examiner's statement that this was a direct, logical, and almost inevitable outcome from the system itself. When the system permits such things to happen, the system should be changed.

A Primary Examiner, with six assistants, is required to act upon six hundred cases per month. Let us do a little arithmetic in this connection. Counting twenty-six working days to the month, six hundred cases per month are more than twenty-three cases per diem. Assuming, that, as implied by the Primary Examiner's phrase, his time is substantially occupied with the general supervision of his class, these twenty-three cases must be handled by the six assistants. This is practically four cases to each assistant each day. The working hours of the Patent Office are from 9 A. M. to 4 P. M., or seven hours per day. This affords less than two hours of one person's time to each case. Under the circumstances the Examiner's excuse, *as an excuse*, was not unreasonable. It may weigh in behalf of the Examiner, but cannot justify the system. Under conditions like those referred to, the wonder is, not that conclusive arguments are disregarded and erroneous actions given, but that chaos, wrong end foremost and upside down, does not reign from one end of the Patent Office to the other. Few men, however capable or however willing, can go on day after day under pressure such as is indicated in this Examiner's statement, and continue to do sound, careful, judicial, and discriminating work during long periods of time. That an Examiner, in order to keep up with his official work, should be compelled to work overtime, to do work at home, is a flagrant imposition upon the official, a detriment to the public service, and, as in the instance just mentioned, the remote source of annoyances and delays to inventors, which are directly contrary to the intent and spirit of the law. The fault, it is manifest, *is inherent in the present system of Examination*, and the remedy is to be found only in a radical modification of the system itself.

Some, not wholly familiar with the subject, may be inclined to suppose, at first blush, that the remedy is an obvious one, and lies in increasing the number of Examiners. This method of meeting the difficulty has been applied, until it has tumbled down by its own weight. The Patent Office, sixty years ago, started with one Examiner. The number has been from time to time increased, until these primary Examiners and assistant Examiners are numbered by scores. Each primary Examiner is practically independent of all the others. Each has his own idea of what does, or does not, constitute patentable novelty. Each has his own favorite forms and formulas of expression. Each his own special knowledge, or the relative want of it, concerning judicial decisions bearing upon the validity of patents ; and each may have his own special degree of inherent reluctance to following any decision of the Commissioner which contravenes an old defect of practice, and each his own, often unconscious, tendency to find reasons for evading or disregarding an interpretation of law or practice which is not coincident with his own ideas. A degree of novelty and utility which satisfies one Examiner of the patentability of inventions, may utterly fail to convince another. There is thus very little uniformity in the ideas of the different divisions of the Patent Office.

The Keynote to Reform.

The first requisite to justice is that there should be a definite and fixed standard by which it may be tested and accorded. In the existing condition of the Patent Office, such a standard as concerns questions of patentable novelty is but remotely approximated. To increase the number of Examiners having the present powers, would be to simply aggravate a state of affairs which is even now in need of speedy and drastic amelioration. With a different and improved method of examining applications, the examining force could be materially and advantageously increased.

If, sixty years ago, the law, instead of instituting official Examinations, had provided for the printing and dissemination of all patents as soon as issued, and left every inventor to investigate the prior state of the art for himself, with liberty to take a patent at his own option and risk, as is done in some European countries, the result would probably have been more satisfactory to inventors, and of more benefit to the public, than the plan that was adopted and still continues in force. It is now, however, quite too late in this country to do away with the Examination of applications antecedent to the issue of patents. To do so would insure a practical illustration of the parable of the wheat and the tares. The destruction of the evil would destroy the good. It is true that a preliminary examination could be made and recorded in connection with the application, leaving the inventor to take the patent if he chose, with the Report of the prior state of the act on file as a notification to the public to qualify any undue breadth in the apparent scope of the patent. One objection to this would be, that it would destroy the presumption of novelty which arises under the present system, and which should, if possible, be preserved. While it would simplify the procedure and obviate many defects, it would not itself be free from many drawbacks. It will, in fact, be difficult to frame a practicable plan for doing way entirely with a quasi-judicial determination of an applicant's rights prior to the issue of a patent to him. Apart from the fact that patents issued without responsible scrutiny would be likely to be broadened beyond legitimate limits, and thus impinge upon public welfare, it is not to be forgotten that the prestige afforded by a governmental Examination affords an additional and substantial money value to a patent, by the presumption of novelty which it *prima facie* affords.

The purpose of any system of Examination is to find, in any given case, the precise line which divides what is new and useful, on the one hand, from what is old and useless on the other. If a patent depart from this line in one direction, the inventor is deprived of that to which legally and morally he is entitled. If error is made in the opposite direction, the public is deprived of that which has already belonged to it and ought not to be taken away. The fallibility of all human agencies will no doubt prevent the attainment of any means for actually ascertaining the proper line of demarcation in all cases, but, as compared with the present practice, very moderate and logical changes may very easily work a most decided improvement.

The general character of those modifications, which would inevitably bring about a change for the better, are so obvious that they were advocated by high authority,—that of the Commissioner already quoted in these pages,—at a time when the need of them was far less than it is now. A quarter of a century ago the Commissioner brought to the notice of Congress a plan of reform which, with modifications in some important respects, goes more directly to the root of the difficulty, and promises more immediate results, with less expense and less departure from established routine, than any other which has been proposed since the origin of the Patent Office.

The fault of the present system is *that in many cases it practically nullifies the direct and only object of the patent law.* This was forcibly set forth, in the report referred to, in these cogent words :

" The theory of the American system is to grant only valid patents, and at a cost so small as to make them obtainable by inventors of very small income. Many inventions, which at first appear very trivial, turn out to be of great value, and others, which at first excite hopes of great value, prove upon trial to be utterly worthless ; undoubtedly very many patents are issued upon inventions having no value to the inventor or anyone else : but experience has shown that such patents do no harm. The theory of our system requires a thorough expert examination before a patent is issued, and a final rejection of all applications that do not present proper matter for valid patents. Many applications embracing important and valuable inventions are accompanied by faulty descriptions, and by claims much broader than the invention—so broad as to invade patents granted to others, and often to cover what is already well known to the public. It is the duty of the Office to ascertain just what is new and useful in the applicant's invention, and then to limit the description and claims to that of which he is really the first inventor."

Having thus stated what a patent ought to be, the same Commissioner proceeded to say why and wherefore it is difficult to make it so. He said :

' Our present system is defective in this : The applicants and their attorneys have direct access to the Examiners. The Examiners determine all questions of fact and of law, and pass cases for issue or reject them. Practically there is no review of their decisions, except as appeals are taken in rejected cases. From their decisions in passing cases for issue, the proceedings being *ex parte*, there is no appeal. The result is, many bad and interfering patents are issued, inventors and manufacturers too often are put to great and needless expense to determine their rights, the public confidence in the Office is diminished, and the validity of all patents issued is suspected."

The system which the head of the Patent Office condemned in these stringent terms a quarter of a century ago, is, as has been already said, that which is still in force in the Patent Office.

In continuation of the paragraph just quoted, this same Commissioner of Patents said :

" To remedy this, I suggest that all authority to pass for issue or reject, be taken away from the Examiners; that they be limited exclusively to the duty of making examinations."

This is the true keynote to all reform in the Patent Office. The reasons for it were sharply defined by the same authority in another paragraph of the same Report. He said :

" 'To examine, for instance, an application for a patent on an improvement in power-looms requires the services of a man who has made power-looms a special study, and is thoroughly familiar with all their perplexing intricacies and thousand forms. To obtain this knowledge requires peculiar taste, close observation, and laborious study.

" To judge correctly of the legal bearing of the facts developed by the examination of such an expert, to correct errors of statement, description, and form, and to determine the intricate legal questions of patentability, abandonment, laches, etc., calls for legal and judicial ability, *and requires different studies and different qualifications.*

" The two offices can be, and I think should be, separated. The Examiner should be just what his title imports, an Examiner, *while the authority to determine legal questions, and to decide as to allowing or rejecting applications, should be left to another tribunal.* Thus, by requiring the action of two officers upon each application, each separated from the other, the most effective check to ignorance, carelessness, and improper influence is secured."

As a matter of exactness in expression, substitute " two tribunals " for " two officers," and the argument is conclusive. To show the convenience with which the examination could be carried on by Examiners segregated from the quasi-judicial duties which now pertain to them, the Commissioner said :

" The records of the Patent Office show that about seven thousand five hundred different things become subjects of application for patents. These seventy-five hundred different subjects, according to their analogies, are thrown into one hundred and forty-five classes.* The one hundred and forty-five classes are assigned to the sixty-six different Examiners in such a manner as to throw classes most nearly analogous together, and at the same time divide the labor as equitably as possible. This arrangement enables each Examiner, if qualified for his place, to become a very competent expert in the classes assigned to him. These one hundred and forty-five classes, I find, can again be reassembled into nine different groups, and still retain in each group so close an analogy, as to make it exceedingly desirable that the classes thus associated should be grouped together in the actual work of making examinations."

To this extent the views of the then Commissioner of Patents are sound and practically indisputable. They comprised facts which were forced upon his attention as soon as he came to the headship of the Patent Office, and he saw the facts and the necessities of the case with the clear vision and thoughtful appreciation of conceded ability. He was, however, new to the intricate details of practice within the Office, and his plan of executive machinery to rectify the mischiefs, which he so distinctly and correctly described, was defective, especially in those portions which related to appeals, and these objections, which were then apparent, have been intensified by subsequent events. So far as I have quoted them, the value of his views has increased with the lapse of time, and constitute apparently the only really available basis for any change for the better in the organization and working of the Patent Office.

Essentials of a Reformed System.

Reform, in its methods, should ordinarily conform as nearly as possible to that which already exists. To utilize what is old, to secure to it a changed function or an increased convenience has, in executive administration, quite as much of merit as can properly be ascribed to absolutely original ideas. To secure efficiency to the work of Examiners, as such, it would be necessary to, first, take

---

* These figures relate, of course, to the classification of twenty-four years ago. They have not diminished in the interval.

from them the labor and responsibility of deciding questions of patentable novelty upon the merits ; and, second, of strictly and more broadly enforcing the rule, already *theoretically* to some slight extent in force, that those references which are the closest to the subject-matter of an application should be cited. Under the existing system, a slip-shod examination may reveal an anticipation of a broad claim, without anticipating minor features and combinations clearly disclosed upon the face of the specification and drawings. Under these circumstances the applicant naturally amends his claim to cover narrower and more specific combinations. Frequently these are met by entirely new references, which, if they had been produced in the first instance, would have shown him the futility of further argument, and saved the Patent Office the trouble of repeated action. The rule should be made imperative that the Examiner should search, *not only for all that may meet the claims*, but for whatever may meet the mechanism, composition of matter, process, or subject-matter, which is disclosed by the *specification* and *drawing*. Such a rule inflexibly carried into effect would tend to diminish rather than increase the labor of examination, and the inventor being informed of the whole state of the art so far as relevant to anything *shown* or *described* in his application, would be enabled to amend or change his specification and claims accordingly.

Under a reformed system, therefore, the work of the Examiners, who could be more properly designated as searchers, would comprise an exhaustive investigation to find whatever should militate against the grant of a patent upon *anything disclosed* in the specification and drawings. A formal statement, setting forth that it embraced the entire state of the art bearing upon the case, and specifying any objections which he might properly urge, should be made over his own signature by the searcher making this examination. A copy of this report should be sent forthwith to the applicant or his authorized representative, and the original, with the application itself, filed before a separate tribunal constituted to consider whether, or to what extent, the results of the search should operate against the grant of the patent. As in many cases the claims would be, to a greater or less extent, anticipated, or the searcher's objections manifestly call for argument, the applicant should be allowed a definite time in which to file amendments and arguments. These should be considered in connection with the searcher's objections, the prior state of the art as disclosed by the search, and the character of the original specification. By this means the tribunal charged with the duty of determining, upon all the facts and circumstances, the matter of patentability, would have the whole case before it in the compact and unembarrassed form most conducive to deliberate consideration and just conclusions.

This tribunal would most logically be constituted by the simple segregation of the Primary Examiners, and their restriction to the semi-judicial duty of determining questions of patentable novelty upon the facts and objections developed by the searchers ; and by separating the latter to the work of searching, and of stating objections, where such appear, to the allowance of a patent upon the invention or any part thereof disclosed in the specification and drawings. By dividing the number of Primary Examiners among the nine (or other appropriate number) divisions, there would be provided to each of the latter a Board of Examiners with the duties mentioned, and the action of these would, in the nature of things, be far more temperate and judicious than has been found possible with Examiners each acting singly by himself and apart from either criticism or co-operation from or with the others. From the decisions of the Board of Examiners for each division, appeals could be taken to the Board of Examiners-in-Chief, in the same manner that they are now taken from actions of Primary Examiners.

Practical Advantages of Reform.

There seems to be no reasonable doubt that the changes proposed would greatly promote the efficiency of the Patent Office in the work for which it was created. It would substitute uniformity of practice in the place of discord. It would utilize one kind and character of talent, the executive, in the work of searching; and another, the judicial, in that of determining patentability upon facts clearly and definitely placed before it ; and would thus utilize both to the highest possible degree. It would obviate the mischiefs which, as shown by the former Commissioner of Patents, were manifest twenty odd years ago, and which are even more obvious and urgent at the present time. It would destroy much of the friction which now attends the working of the patent system, and would annihilate the arbitrary authority (which is too great to be properly confided to any subordinate) that now inheres in each primary Examiner, and which, though in many instances exercised wisely and conscientiously, may, in the hands of an unscrupulous, careless, or incompetent Examiner be used to inflict irreparable injury upon deserving and innocent inventors, and result in denying rights to which, under the law, an applicant may be entitled.

Whether any or many, or none or all, of such Examiners are now in the Patent Office is a question to which it is no part of the purpose of these pages to reply, but in this connection , there may be quoted from the Report of the Commissioner the emphatic and suggestive words on a like topic, as follows :

" Errors of judgment and susceptibility to temptation are incident to human nature ; and, whatever may be the checks and guards, their ugly forms will occasionally crop out in all positions of public or private trust."

In conclusion : As the proposed changes, with all their manifest advantages, will not imperatively require an increase in the working force of the Patent Office, and will not necessarily involve any additional expense,—as they will confide to the Assistant Examiners the work to which they have been accustomed, and will promote the Primary Examiners to the unembarrassed discharge, under more favorable conditions, of the more elevated of the duties in which they have acquired experience,—it is difficult to perceive wherein reasonable objection can be made to the proposed reform. It is true that an obstinate conservatism may, and often does, hinder and delay changes the utility of which is manifest. It has been so more than once in the history of the Patent Office. For example, during many years a model was required with each and every application. The average expense of these has been estimated at twenty-five dollars each, and this estimate is probably too low rather than too high. It was an onerous tax upon inventors and upon developing and progressive industries. Probably not less than ten millions of dollars were thus uselessly taken from the pockets of inventors prior to the time when the requirement was abolished. Successive Commissioners and a majority of Examiners held, year after year, that examinations could not be adequately conducted without models. Yet, during more than a dozen years past, models have been dispensed with by the Patent Office. The examinations are more conveniently made without them, and an attorney who would now insist upon sending a model with each case filed by him would be regarded as a nuisance, and would be promptly told to stop. The time may not be remote when, similarly, the present methods of examination and its concomitants will be regarded with wonder and surprise that they were permitted to remain so long.

APPENDIX.

What Inventors Should Bear in Mind at the Start.

THE evolution of an invention follows a natural and definite course. This is so inevitable that it controls the routine of proof in all questions of alleged priority, whether in the courts or in the Patent Office.

An invention implies in its essence the creation of something new and original. In any case, the query is likely to arise, When did this creation begin? or as phrased in Patent Office parlance, " What was the date of the conception of the invention? "

Merely conceiving an invention, and stopping with that, cannot benefit the public, and consequently ought not to benefit the inventor. The law offers the inventor a patent with a view to a subsequent advantage to the public. Therefore, to entitle him to protection he must do more than think ; he must act. The first thing to do with an idea of a new improvement is to show it in some form, so that its nature may be made manifest to others. Where it can be graphically shown, the first and most natural means to this end is a simple sketch. When a sketch can only partially disclose the invention, or when, as with a process, it may not be capable of showing it at all, a written description is the obvious substitute. Such a sketch or drawing should always be dated. What was the date of your first sketch ? is an important question which is almost always asked of an inventor when the history of his improvement comes to the fore.

While the unsupported testimony of one person may sometimes carry persuasive weight, it is always better when that testimony is supported by others, or by circumstances which confirm it. When did you first communicate your invention to others ? is a query asked quite as frequently as any other. The inventor should take an early opportunity of explaining his invention confidentially to

23

one or more trusty acquaintances. This, ordinarily, is most conveniently done by showing a sketch. The date is very frequently fixed in such cases by having the parties witness the sketch, and affixing the date in their own hand-writing.

When the idea had been formulated into what the inventor believes to be a practically successful shape, he should either have careful drawings made, or should make a model. This shows intention to perfect the invention, and persistence in developing the idea. Means should be taken to record the date of the completion of the drawing, or model, as the case may be. In some cases a model may so nearly approach the character of a working machine, or a finished device, as to almost or even quite reach the character of a completed invention.

The next and conclusive step is the "reduction to practice"; in other words, the actual construction and operation of the machine or device, the actual using, in a practical way, of a method or process. This should be done under circumstances which admit of proof. Filing an application for a patent is substantially an equivalent for reduction to practice, unless the attendant circumstances are very unusual. A patent may be taken on an invention that has not been actually constructed, or used, or practically tested, provided that, as shown and described, the invention is capable of practical use. Patents are granted for the *disclosure* of improvements, and when an inventor, by filing an application, has disclosed an actually useful invention to the Patent Office, it should not be necessary that he shall have previously demonstrated its usefulness by putting it into operation. The course of an inventor should be determined by circumstances. If the invention is a simple one, or if he have excellent facilties for testing it, he should put the improvement to an experimental test before filing the application. Frequently in such cases further improvements and modifications are suggested, which may be incorporated in the same patent. When the expense of actual working may be considerable, when the inventor is convinced of the utility of the invention without subjecting it to actual use, or where he has any especial reason for haste, he may file his application forthwith, and put the invention into actual operation at a more convenient season.

In cases of Interference in the Patent Office, an advantage lies with the application which has been filed first. The presumption is in favor of the first comer, and the application which is filed latest has the burden of disproving or overcoming that presumption.

In the case of interfering applications for patents, the question of diligence is of the highest importance. An inventor who is the first to conceive the invention, the first to make a sketch of it, and the first to disclose it to another, and yet dawdles and dallies and delays without strong and valid reasons for so doing, will be beaten by an adversary who had been diligent in pursuing the idea to a practical end, either by actual reduction to practice or by filing an application for a patent in which it is shown in useful and operative form.

When an inventor believes that further improvement is necessary or desirable to bring his invention into operative condition, and yet wishes to shut off others in the meantime from getting a patent on the same idea, he may file a caveat. This does not, as is sometimes supposed, afford protection after the manner of a patent, but simply entitles an inventor, during a year after filing the caveat, to notice from the Patent Office in case another party files an application for a patent on the same invention. Upon receipt of such notice he must, to preserve his rights, file an application within a certain stated time and go into Interference with the other applicant. Caveats are very useful in exceptional cases, but they cannot take the place of formal applications for patents. Ordinarily, it is better to file an application for a patent in the first instance, unless the invention is in a very incomplete condition, or unless there are special reasons for delay and for further experiment.

As a general rule, an inventor should carefully preserve everything that relates to the history of his invention. It takes but a few minutes to make a pencil sketch, and only a few seconds to mark its date upon it. Sketches, drawings, models, experimental machines and parts thereof, should be kept in such a manner that each may be positively and easily identified. Many inventors keep a regular record of their novel ideas, experiments, etc. This plan is a very advantageous one. It not only preserves the facts concerning inventions which become successful, but also causes many transitory ideas, which may contain the germs of profitable inventions, from being forgotten.

Why Inventors Should be Diligent.   A Recent Decision.

The statute forbids the issue of a patent upon an invention which has been in public use more than two years prior to the application. This has been generally understood to mean that an inventor may make, use, and sell the invention for any length of time, less than two years, before applying for a patent.   This seems to the writer to be the true and (with all due respect for the Court) the " common-sense " view of the intent of the statute.   However, a novel, or at least a different, interpretation of the law, has, as recently as January last, been taken by the U. S. Circuit Court, for the District of Nebraska.   The suit in which this decision was rendered was brought upon a patent, the specification of which stated upon its face as follows :

" The invention is in practical operation and on the market it considerable numbers, and the facts here stated with regard to its operation are such as have been ascertained from commercial experience with it."

In support of its conclusion the Court quoted from an opinion of the United States Supreme Court, as follows :

" An abandonment of an invention to the public may be evinced by the conduct of the inventor at any time, even within the two years named in the law."

The Court, after making this citation from the Superior Tribunal, continued :

" It is clear that if made to appear that, before filing an application for a patent, the inventor had abandoned the invention to the public, the patent, if issued, will be held invalid.   Upon the face of the patent now under consideration, it appears that, previous to the date of the filing of the application, the inventor had put the invention into practical operation ; that a considerable number of mills embodying the improvement had been put upon the market for sale ; and that the facts recited in the application, as evidence of the value and usefulness of the combination, had been ascertained from commercial experience with it.   These statements preclude the idea that the use made was experimental.   The recitals show that the invention or combination had been perfected so as to make it practical. Numbers of mills had been put upon the market, and upon the knowledge derived from this extensive commercial use, the patentees relied for proof of the successful working of the combination. Certainly, the facts thus stated by the applicant are strong evidence of abandonment. If an inventor, after perfecting his invention, places it upon the market in large or considerable numbers, and sells to all who desire to purchase, and continues to do so for months, without applying for a patent, no other conclusion can be drawn than that he does not intend to apply for a patent ; and he cannot be permitted, after having made public the knowledge of his invention, and induced many persons to purchase, to then conclude that the invention may be worth patenting, and that he will debar the public from using the knowledge they have acquired from him, by·procuring the issuance of a patent."

This language, forcible as it is, was coupled with a slender qualification, as follows :

" It is well settled that delay in applying for a patent may be explained, and be excused, by reason of sickness or inability to furnish the means needed to procure a patent, and also a sale, or sales, may be made under circumstances which are not inconsistent with an intent to apply for a patent. Primarily, the defense of abandonment is based upon matters of fact, and each case will depend upon the facts proven therein ; the legal conclusions being that if, in fact, the inventor did abandon his invention to the public, then he cannot afterward obtain a valid patent therefor."

The plain conclusion is, that while there may be cases in which manufacture, use, and sale on a commercial scale within the limit of · two years prior to the application may be explained away, the practice is an exceedingly dangerous one. That the use prior to application should not, in general, be permitted to reach commercial proportions, and that when the inventor has once satisfied himself by trial within the limits of experiment that his invention is a valuable one, the sooner he applies for his patent the better.

Some General Rules that May be Observed with Advantage.

As applications, in the vast majority of cases, are prepared, filed, and prosecuted through attorneys, it is unnecessary to here remark at length upon the essentials of a properly prepared case.

There are, however, a few simple rules the uniform observance of which tend greatly to promote an inventor's welfare. Among them :

Always carefully explain the invention *in detail* to your patent agent or attorney. It is his business to put the inventor's ideas into legal and technical form. He cannot fully do this unless he fully understands the invention, its various uses, its modifications, if such there be, the difference between it and other inventions for a like purpose, so far as known to the inventor, and the advantages derived or expected from its use.

Never sign a specification (nor anything else) until you have read it from beginning to end, and understand it thoroughly. Do not sign or execute applications in blank, *i. e.*, petition, power, and oath, with the idea that the specification may be subsequently supplied.

In selecting an attorney seek one of approved experience and established repute. Act toward him with the same propriety and fairness that you, yourself, desire from those with whom you do business, and if at any time, after affording fair opportunity for explanation, you have reasonable cause to distrust either his integrity or his competence, close your relations with him and go somewhere else. An honorable attorney has no difficulty in keeping his record straight, for the file-wrapper and contents of every application show precisely what has been done, and when and how it has been done, at every step in the history of the case from the hour when it was originally filed.

Remember that while you are justified in expecting that your attorney will prepare and push your application with skill, care, and discretion, you should also bear in mind that no attorney can work miracles. If an invention is actually anticipated by proper references,—prior inventions or devices previously known in the art,—the Patent Office can have no legal right to allow a patent upon it. In such cases the Examiner is in duty bound to reject your application, and your attorney has no right to insist that he do otherwise. The attorney may and should, and you should lend him your willing assistance in so doing, *seek for sound distinctions* between the *references* and the *invention*, so that the claims may be amended to cover whatever you may be actually entitled to, although it may not be as much as you originally expected. Many patents with narrow claims have proved to be of great financial value, although, obviously, when the invention is meritorious, the broader the claim the greater the value of the patent.

It is well, also, to appreciate the fact that cases are of every-day

If, as sometime occurs, you, as an inventor, find yourself at a disadvantage in making money from your improvements, it may be advisable to seek and find some acute and honest man whose business abilities and experience may be fairly offset against the originative and creative faculty which makes you an inventor. Accord him the same liberality in the use of your inventive skill that you expect from him in the use of his money, and with him go ahead with promptness, energy, and confidence in whatever your own unbiased and deliberate judgment has approved. There are, of course, many people, and many conditions, to which this advice will not apply, but that two heads are better than one has often been demonstrated, when one of them belonged to a man of genius who could invent, and the other to a man of talent who could master the intricacies and difficulties of business affairs. Do not lose courage under the usual and inevitable trials of an inventor's life, and do not throw away a good chance for a problematical possibility of a better one. Undertakings based upon patents have their risks. So have all other forms of human endeavor. But there is no reason to doubt that more and greater fortunes have been made, either directly or indirectly, from inventions than from any one other department of business enterprise based upon moderate investments of capital. Remember that improvement in every branch of production is progressive ; that an invention which to-day may stand at the very head of an industry may to-morrow be superseded by one invented hundreds or thousands of miles away by some person of whom you have never heard. Such are the chances, and such the opportunities, afforded in the realm of invention, and in that realm, as in others of business effort, there is always room at the top—fortune, fame, and success, as the reward of persevering and well-directed thought and indomitable energy.

FINIS.

www.ingramcontent.com/pod-product-compliance
Lightning Source LLC
Chambersburg PA
CBHW032144080426
42733CB00008B/1200